THE ART OF
SEGRELLES

THE ART OF SEGRELLES

NANTIER·BEALL·MINOUSTCHINE
Publishing co.
new york

ARTIST'S NOTES FOR THE FANS

Often, aspiring artists and even pros ask me how I work. I thought it would be worthwhile to offer some insight into the way I do my illustrations.

The originals are done with oil paint on paper. To the unitiated, this may seem obvious, but in fact paper can only be used with a coat of waterproofing. In fact, with this waterproofing, I've even been able to use rag paper.

Obviously, artists do not all use the same techniques. From the start, one must assume that the ends will justify the means. The best technique to use should ultimately be the ones the artist experiments with and finds most suitable to his or herself so as to reach the desired effect. For me, oil on paper has been the best medium.

At first, I fix the paper on a board with tape along the edges. Then I waterproof it with latex. The paper will swell with the water but does stretch back taught on the board while drying. I start with a rough using crayons, then begin the painting only in a very sketchy fashion, choosing my colors and placing them in dabs onto the paper. I work with cobalt secative so that the paint will not dry by the next day.

When I have to do a first draft for the client to accept, I will give this first step more work for a more finished look; but even without that, I need to go through this very necesary rough beginning for myself at first. It's necessary that the colors be very compact so as to make sure one cannot distinguish the brush strokes, even though I work with very thin layers of color.

One of the main advantages with my technique is that if a portion does not please me, I can erase it with a rag while still leaving intact my initial pencils which are protected by the latex.

After my first layers of color are dry, I put in the detail as needed. I then let that dry and I varnish it. This is another important step as it unifies all hues, especially those which become mat as they dry, and gives them all their true intensity.

At that point I add with tempera or plastic any hard light sources or extra sparkle that may be needed as well as any detail which I cannot do with oil.

Finally, I cut the margins of the paper leaving some white border and I cover the whole with a sheet of tracing paper to protect it. The job is done and ready for the printer.

This book presents only a small number of my illustrations. The choice is made keeping to a fantasy theme. I'll provide brief comments for each as I think that will help art lovers to better understand my work process.

1. This painting was commissioned by an American publisher. As all originals made for the USA, it was done in a very large format so as to be able to include more detail in the final reproduction.

2. On this work, note the complete absence of strong colors on the bird in the background. That further emphasizes the foreground. The original is 11" by 20" which is roughly the usual size for European covers. This was used as the cover of The Mercenary # 3 in the USA (the original hardcover version).

3. American wrap-around cover of 28" by 20". The commission asked for themes and objects of the Celtic civilization. An illustrator must have documentation on the widest variety of subjects or else he's in trouble.

4. I'm particularly proud of this illustration as I did it entirely from my own mind's eye. Illustrators often use models and photos, but personally, I believe they should be used only for general inspiration. One cannot be tied to them. That's why the less I use them, the more proud I'll be of my work.

5. As much as this is an illustration of fantasy, this cover still stays within the bounds of the logical. I respect reality as much as possible by drawing the reptile's head as it is and by creating wide wings. An illustrator must observe all details.

6. This is an old double page illustration. As I mentioned before, the ends justify the means: I must admit that the fly's hairs were done with a ball point pen.

7. An American cover where you can see the first stage of my work in the mountain range in the background which I purposefully did not cover up in the second stage as I thought the effect to be satisfying.

8. An illustration done specially for Germany. It's done from imagination and I want to bring attention to the importance I bring in doing metal, glass, or other shiny surfaces. A little dash of paint in just the right place can be just the right thing.

9. Spectacular wrap-around American cover on a fantasy theme filled with light and a certain mood. I try to achieve this kind of mix and effect as often as I can and as much as a commission will allow. A good sense of perspective is needed for this.

10. An American cover for a children's book. The anecdote here is that the man with the hen is me, a little older but with more hair. When I was drawing the boy, I had trouble with the mouth, so I asked my daughter to give me a surprised look: another trick of the pro.

11. Under water cover illustration. Often, very diluted oil paint can produce interesting effects. What's important is that one has to know when to stop. Look at the ground the warrior is on: the oil is nothing but white spirit and just a hint of color.

12. For this original, I worked a long time before getting the right color for the chariot. The background forces one to study such details so as to avoid chromatic dissonance.

13. The hard part in this American commission was doing the structure of the boat. The challenge was to enrich it with authentic details. Perspective here also was a challenge: I had to pencil the entire boat with each point's line to the horizon.

14. This cover is part of a series done for Germany. All have a young girl in front. For the foreground, I used models or photos to obtain better realism.

15. This is from the first album of THE MERCE-NARY. The whole graphic novel series is done in oil. For this drawing, I cut out all the foreground portions with a regular pen, a method I quickly had to drop.

16. An American cover with the light behind the character which helped me give depth to the picture.

17. Wrap-around cover for a Mercenary graphic novel version in Europe. All you see came out of my imagination except the girl where I used a model. I also created the armor in my head, albeit inspired by one which I have at home. What's important is to give the impression the armor can actually work and to add real details, even if they may seem superfluous.

18. A German cover. Notice that in spite of all the different elements mixed in, the light always comes from the same direction.

19. Fantasy and Science Fiction for the USA. Note that proper use of shading can contribute to the mood.

20. This wrap-around cover for America was particularly demanding for all its different sources of light. Such work demands a careful tracing in perspective and a great deal of thought in communicating its very special ambience.

21. Illustration for America which had very specific demands from the start. A case where the illustrator must follow exacting specifications. Even then, a professional must enrich the theme and give it strength.

22. Cover for Great Britain. One of many I've done for that country. I've illustrated novels by Alistair Mclean and Desmond Bagley among others, on themes of action, murder-mystery and adventure.

23. Another work for England. Commissions from that country are generally quite specific. They even send me rough drafts at times. For such commissions I normally have to have my first color draft approved before proceeding.

24. Cover done without specific commission. In such cases, you can draw whatever you want without fear of what artistic directors might think. I did this from my imagination entirely with tricks one learns from years of experience. The sea fascinates me. I love its polished and undulating surface which reflects the colors around it.

25. Vignette from THE MERCENARY # 3. The hero must get in a palace protected by an enormous spider's web littered with bodies of warriors. There's only a small door which is guarded by an enormous sea monster...

26. Light, mystery, fantasy... a wealth of richness of color is necessary. Pink and orange hues would do well here... these are my thought processes as I work.

27. Illustration for my SEAWORLDS portfolio. There are little details which at first may seem trivial. However, without them, something would be missing. The transparent fingernails contribute to the light effect. The water reflects the colors around it with varying intensity. A deep sea may be almost black but it will still reflect hues. The sea is never the same and is quite a challenge to paint, but there are tricks.

28. Also from the SEAWORLDS portfolio. The light source is from above with reflections in the shadows. When one draws something that does not exist, one needs to think it out logically. Even though this is fantasy, physical laws of the universe are still in effect. If you create light, you have to think of its shadow and its reflections. If you draw matter, you must think out its texture. Note the slight transparence of the eel-like creature.

29. This cover underwent many revisions. The original was painted over three times. The first with another horrible monster in the background, the second to cover the girl because of censorship, and the third to uncover her yet again!.

THE MERCENARY by Vicente Segrelles

© Vicente Segrelles controlled by NORMA
© NBM for the English translation 1987
NBM
35-53 70th St.
Jackson Heights, NY 11372
Ask for our complete color catalog of graphic novels.
Printed in Spain by NORMA Serveis Gràfics
Tx 50293 - Fax (343) 2323654 ☎ 245 64 03